PTANG STUDIO LTD

HOME DECOR

PTANG STUDIO LTD

HOME DECOR

LOFT

HOME DECOR Ptang Studio Ltd.

Editor:
Loft Publications
Art Director:
TRAMA, Estudi Gràfic, S.C.P.
Graphic Design and Layout:
Nacho Gracia Blanco
Cover Design:
Nacho Gracia Blanco

© 2012 Loft Publications

Loft Publications, S. L.
Via Laietana, 32, 4º, of. 92
08003 Barcelona, España
Tel.: +34 932 688 088
Fax: +34 932 687 073
loft@loftpublications.com
www.loftpublications.com

ISBN: 978-84-9936862-7
D.L.: B-00845-2012

All rights reserved. No part of this book may be used or reproduced in any manner whatsoever without written permission except in the case of brief quotations embodied in critical articles and reviews.

Attempts have been made to identify and contact copyright owners. Errors or omissions will be corrected in future editions.

CONTENTS

Introduction

PTang Studio Ltd is an architectural and interior design firm that was founded in 1999 in Hong Kong. The firm has undergone rapid growth in recent years, going from the initial sole proprietorship structure to that of a partnership.

The firm currently features architects specialized in different areas of the profession and in interior design. This structure makes it possible for the firm to take on projects of different scale and type, enabling it to benefit from the variety and diversity of its work.

As shown by the projects included in this collection, the work done by our firm comes under two general categories: residential and corporate. Our residential projects include small and medium-scale apartments, and model apartments to show prospective occupants. The commercial side takes in everything from large-scale projects like corporate headquarters to luxury suites and temporary executive accommodation in hotels and apartment buildings.

PTang Studio Ltd designs spaces to provide the most comfortable surrounds for our clients based on their individual needs and tastes. Our designs are focused on maximum quality and innovation, and are imbued with a unique style that mixes modern luxury with a forward-looking sophistication that transcends the boundaries of current design.

The energy and dynamism transmitted by the designers, whose careers have given them broad experience in all aspects of the profession, enable them to offer clients the best possible service.

PTang Studio Ltd is one of the most prestigious architectural and design firms operating in China. It has reaped a large number of acknowledgements since 2005, such as the IAI Award, the IIDA Global Excellence Award, and the Asia Pacific Residential Property Awards, and its name has also been gaining in strength on the international scene.

The pages of this book contain a broad sample of the firm's most representative projects featuring their fresh and unique style, an unmistakable sign of their identity present in all their work.

Residential

Anglers' Bay

Bel-Air on the Peak Show Flat

Carmen's Garden

Grand Promenade

Hereford Road Residence

Hillsborough Court

La Rossa Show Flat

Lyttelton Road

No. 8 Tai Tam

Parc Palais

Sukhothai Residences

Anglers' Bay

Sham Tseng | Hong Kong
Area: 680 sq ft

A white colour scheme is featured in this apartment throughout its walls and tiles, mixing minimalism with a "cyber" theme, which is enhanced through the use of materials such as glass and plastic. Most of the furniture is transparent and futuristic. Muted tones have been used in the bedroom where the two original rooms have been merged and are now separated from the living area by a rotating cabinet mounted with a plasma TV. This allows the dwellers to enjoy their favourite shows from either the bedroom or the living room by just turning the cabinet.

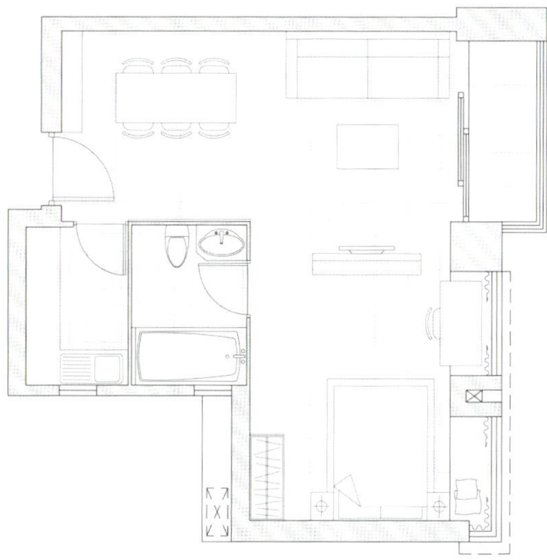

Floor plan

Bel-Air on the Peak Show Flat

Island South | Hong Kong
Area: 2400 sq ft

Clean and tidy are the adjectives to describe this flat. This 2400-sq-ft dwelling has no large storage cabinets, just simple, small-scale furniture, giving the owner a highly flexible space. Black and white always form magical combinations and serve as a great background for colourful artwork and accessories.

The black wallpaper with horizontal strips visually reduces the length of the corridor and forms a great contrast with the bright living area. The colours combined in the bedrooms – white and grey – form less of a contrast and create a harmonic atmosphere for resting.

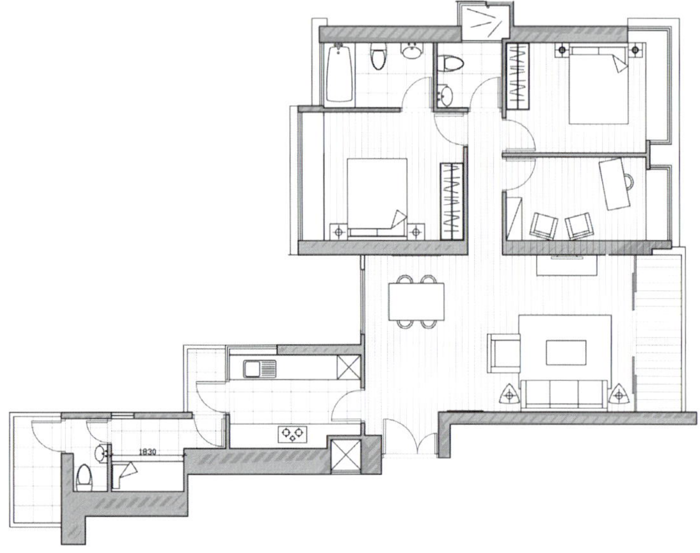

Floor plan

Carmen's Garden

Jordon | Hong Kong
Area: 1010 sq ft

This two-bedroom apartment stands out for its daring dark look. Upon entering, an oval marble dining table with a strong texture quickly becomes the focal point of the flat. Different kinds of pendant lamps, wall lamps and ceiling fans form an interesting and contrasting colour scheme.

Purple walls match with dark walnut furniture in the master bedrooms creating a comfortable resting environment. In the study, the designer has used silver and grey to make an energetic and bright space. This strong contrast makes the whole flat a dramatic living space.

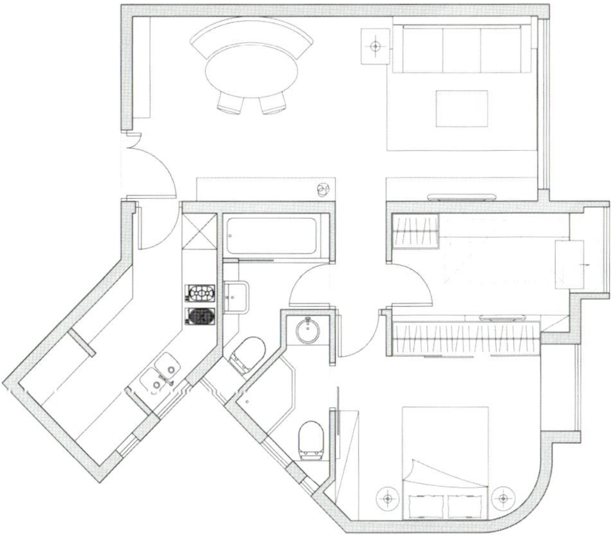

Floor plan

Grand Promenade

Island East | Hong Kong
Area: 1300 sq ft

The designer decided to go for an all-black look for the three-bedroom apartment: quite a daring theme. From the entrance, the eye is immediately drawn to a dramatic space housing a white curvy sculpture, accentuated by spotlights in a black mirrored cabinet.

Black walls contrast starkly against the tan wooden floor, the deep grains of which almost map out the path down the hallway and into the living area of the home. Another unique area created by the designer is the wall of photographs facing the dining area. He also took pains to balance simple, streamlined furnishings with funkier items.

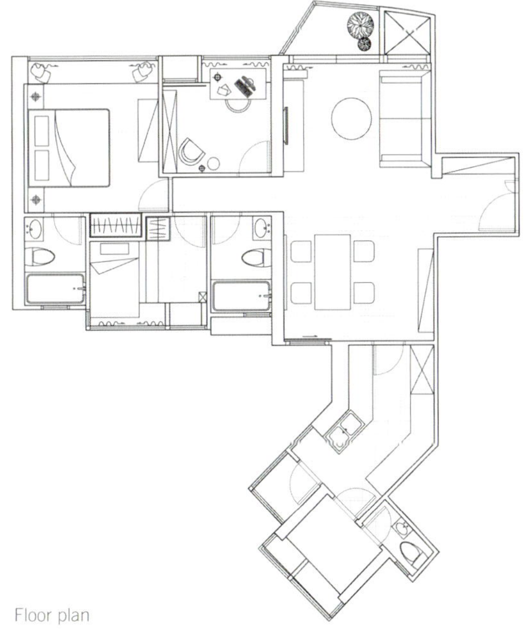

Floor plan

SAMSUNG

Hereford Road Residence

Hereford Road | Hong Kong
Area: 2500 sq ft + 2000 sq ft garden

Located in an area of low-rise buildings, the flat enjoys sunlight throughout the day so the designer decided to use darker colours. The only metal element in the flat is a big bronze cupboard that imbues the flat with a cool and shiny feeling.

Several materials are used in one area, including metal, wood, wallpaper and leather. The designer has used a waved pattern to connect all these elements together to form a harmonic atmosphere. It also visually elongates and heightens the ceiling of the flat.

In the bedrooms, an even darker colour tone is used to match with the mirrored walls. They create a comfortable place to relax and rest.

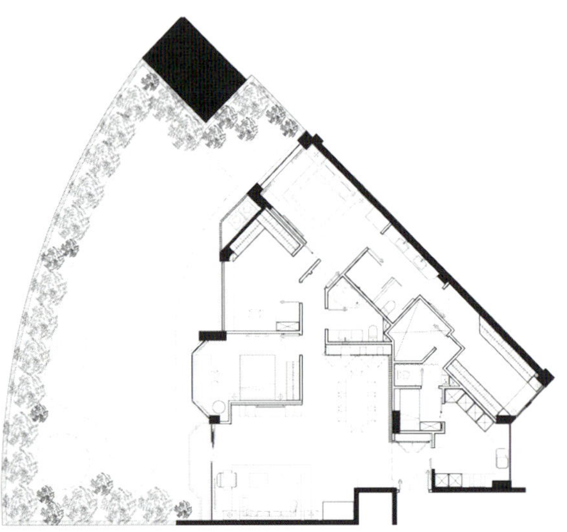

Floor plan

Hillsborough Court

Old Peak Road | Hong Kong
Area: 850 sq ft

The owner does not need much storage space in the flat, as he is a frequent traveller, which gave the designer a great deal of flexibility when designing the flat. The theme chosen is based on natural elements and the colour green, so there are many tree features in the flat.

The designer removed the wall between the living room and study, replacing it with a glass partition with a tree image. The bookcase comprises green and white storage boxes, forming a wall that is a central feature in the flat. Together with the green boxes in the living room, the flat is full of colours and layers.

In the master bedroom, a white wardrobe with tree graphics and a wooden table form a perfect resting space.

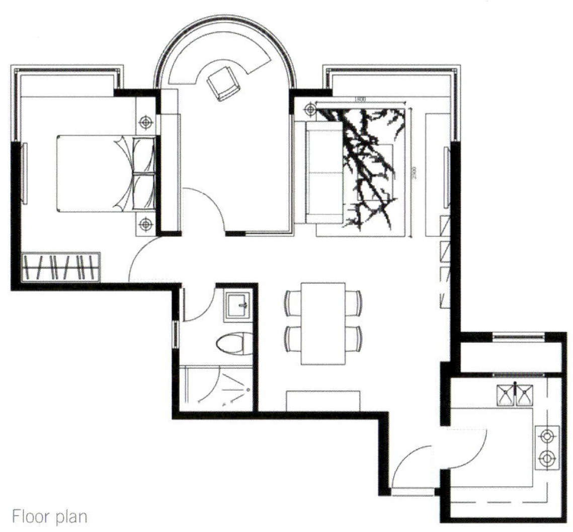

Floor plan

PLASTIC DESIGN

La Rossa Show Flat

Tung Chung | Hong Kong
Area: 1000 sq ft

Stylish red and pure white form the backbone of the design scheme. Floral graphics around the home create a warm atmosphere in this three-bedroom unit with sea views. A red TV cabinet acts like a red carpet, contrasting with the tree wall graphic, making this square-shaped living room a romantic space.

A tree-like bookshelf in the study is not only highly functional, but also a focal point of the dwelling. Its grey square boxes and big red translucent flower on the door create a dramatic contrast.

In the master bedroom, bedding, wallpaper and the wardrobe doors are covered in flowers, continuing the central floral theme.

and Reflections

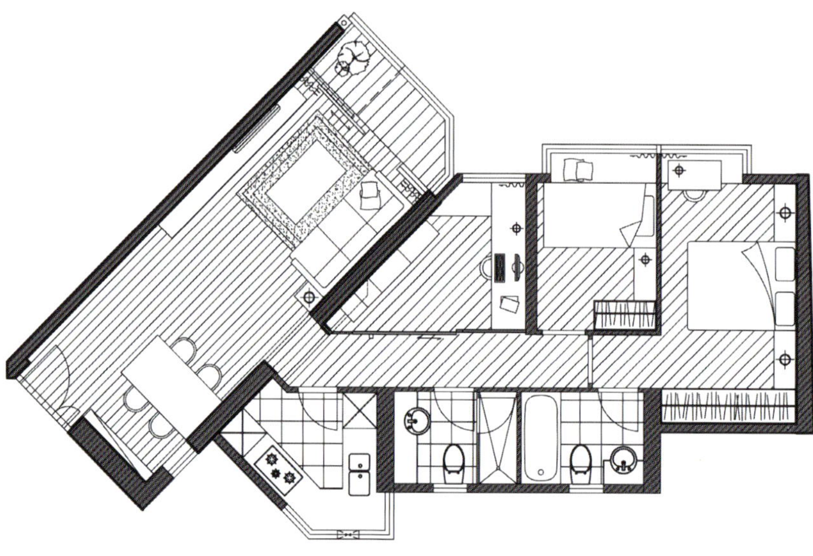

Floor plan

Lyttelton Road

Mid-Levels | Hong Kong
Area: 1400 sq ft + 1400 sq ft roof top

This is a flat with a perfectly proportioned open-plan space with a large roof top. Being minimalists at heart, the clients gave the designer a clear and simple brief for their home: it should be white and bright. Minimalist interiors, when stylishly executed, actually have a lot to offer.

While white surfaces dominate, varied textures and, more importantly, good quality materials, are used to evoke different inviting ambiences, ranging from soft. and comfortable to cool and crisp.

As befits the simple colour palette, there are few accessories, which would seem redundant or might even create a feeling of clutter. Instead, a few lively Shanghai Tan cushions and throws punctuate the space with just the right amount of interest and colour.

The sliding doors in the kitchen allow plenty of light to enter the living area and visually divide the apartment's different zones while also serving to contain cooking odours, a necessary element given that the homeowners are avid chefs.

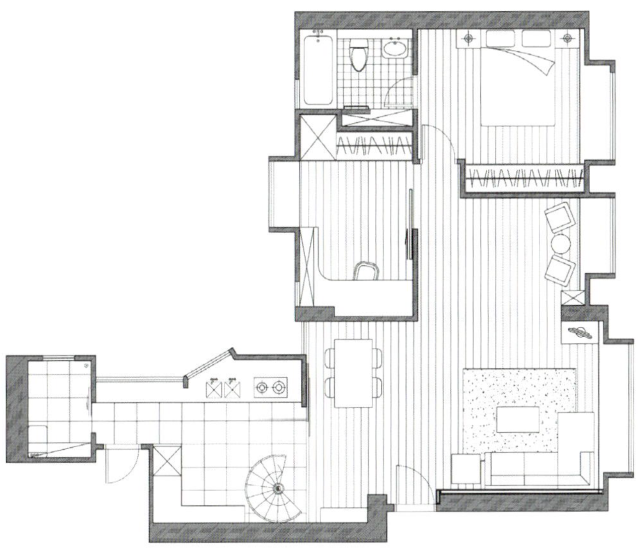

Floor plan

No. 8 Tai Tam

Island South | Hong Kong
Area: 8500 sq ft + 4500 outdoor garden + pool

The design of this 8500 sq ft house incorporates a few classic elements with contemporary touches. For example, the house features many black walls – a detail the homeowners specifically requested, because they felt black was synonymous with class. For these walls, the designer chose wallpapers and drapes with somewhat traditional motifs, such as floral patterns, and combined them with furnishings and accessories with distinctly sleek, streamlined silhouettes.

The designers also made the most of the home's distinguishing features. The basement floor extends onto the deck, featuring a private infinity pool, which, at certain times of the day, didn't actually receive much sunlight. To counteract this problem, the designer punched a hole through the floor of the spacious terrace above and paved it with glass, thereby creating an enormous skylight.

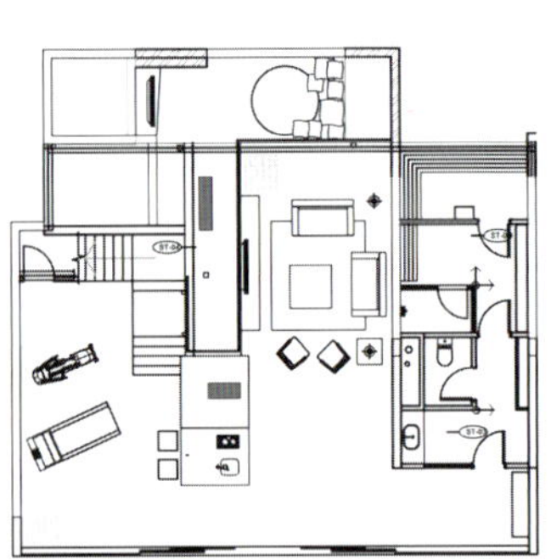

Pool side function room

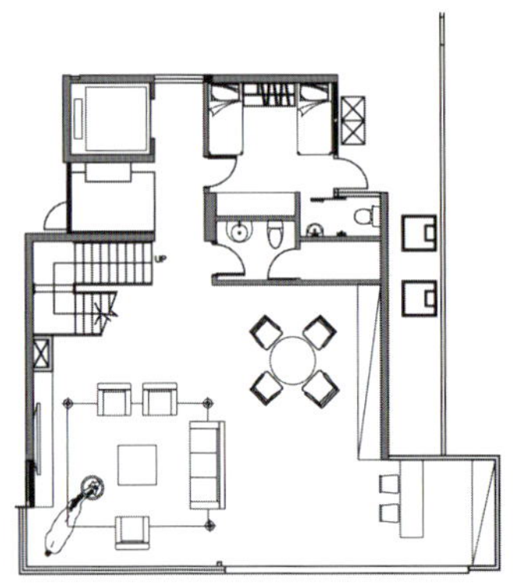

Ground floor

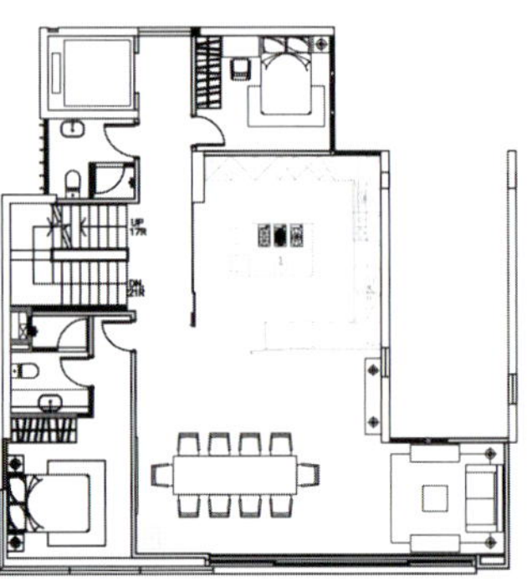

First floor

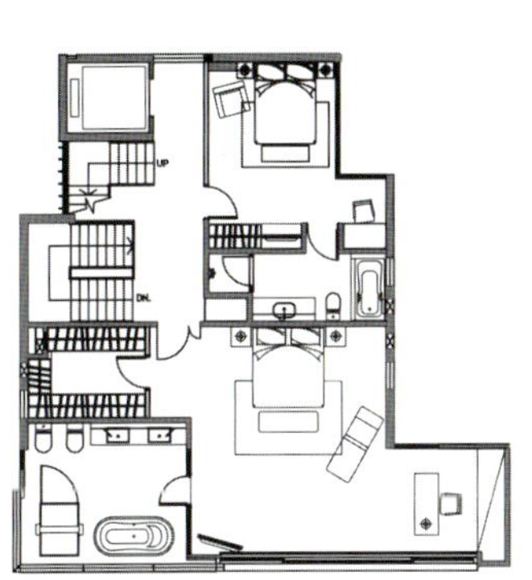

Second floor

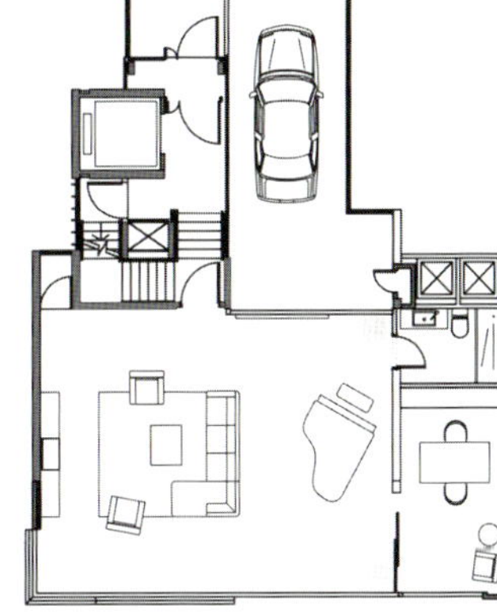

Third floor

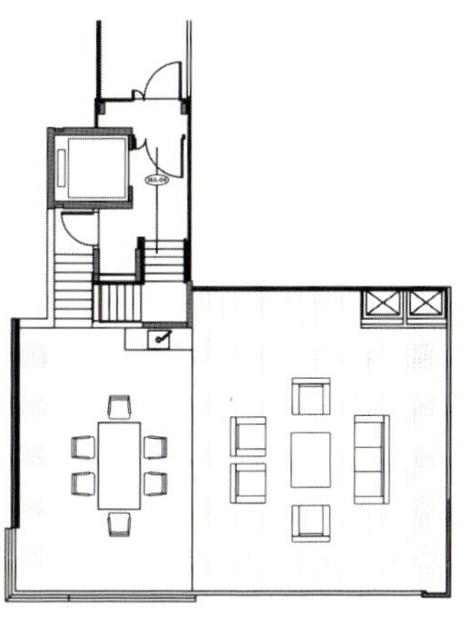

Roof floor

Parc Palais

Ho Man Tin | Hong Kong
Area: 2800 sq ft + 1400 sq ft roof garden

When entering the household, the eyes are stretched up towards the soaring height of the ceilings by the intricate laser-cut 3D layered wall that is truly majestic in scale. The designers came up with white-on-white graphics to soften the space. Otherwise, such a large expanse of plain wall, together with the huge glass windows, could look stark and cold.

The design requirement was simple – to keep the home minimal and white, and to bring out its sense of space. That was one of the greatest challenges, as the space could have appeared too empty. The designer therefore added colourful, contemporary furnishings to jazz up the muted hues.

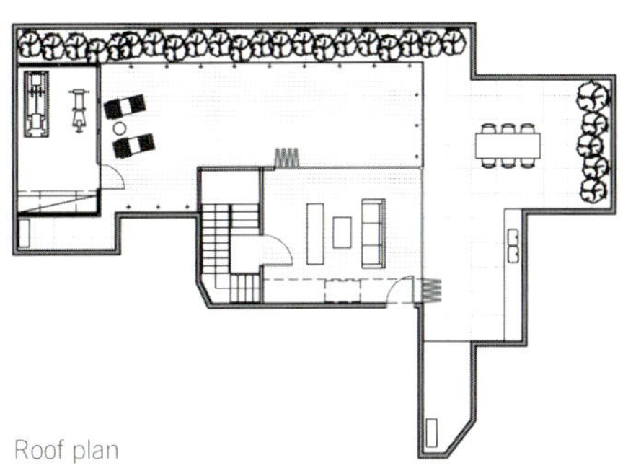

Roof plan

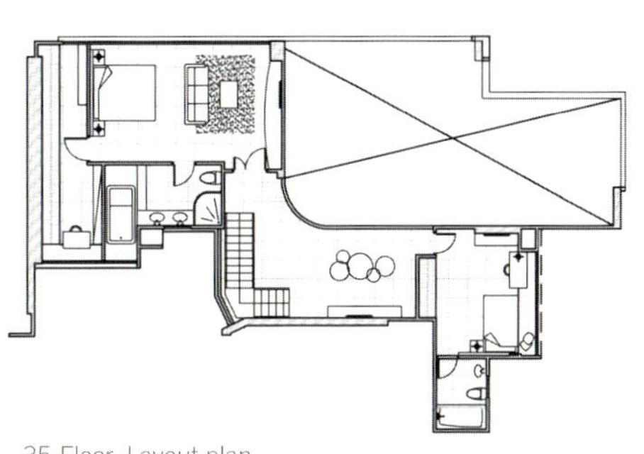

35 Floor. Layout plan

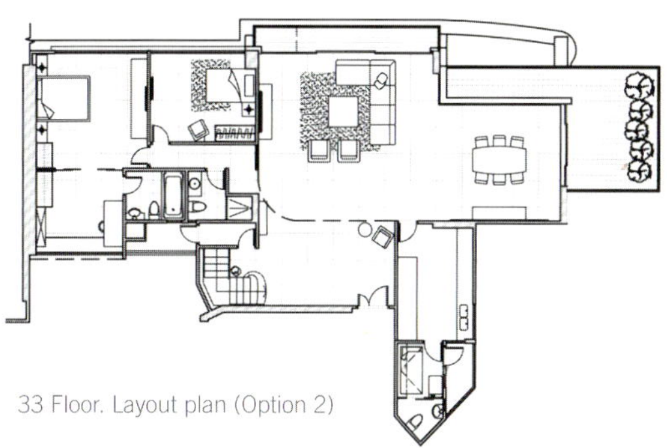

33 Floor. Layout plan (Option 2)

Sukhothai Residences

Bangkok | Thailand
Area: 2000 sq ft

Designers tried to play-up the double-height space by visually and physically connecting the levels with the help of wallpaper and artwork.

To enrich the texture in the box-like flat, the designers added silk panels, teak frames, stone and wood flooring, and glass items. Moreover, furniture of different shapes and colors create a cozy room.

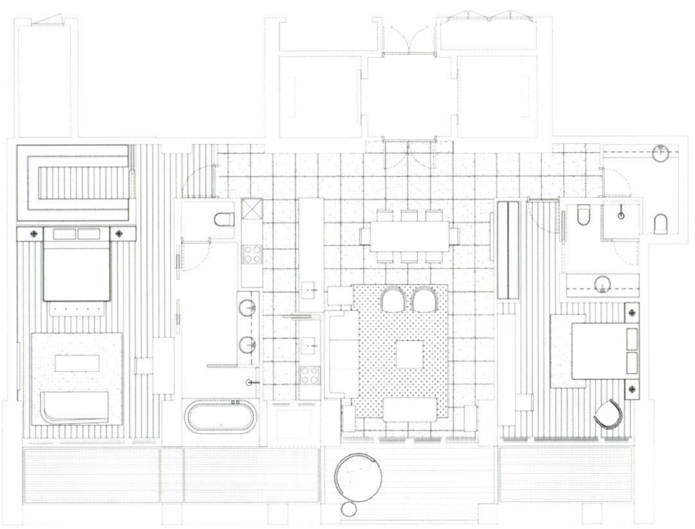

Floor plan

Commercial

Hill Paramount

Le Bleu Deux Show Flat - Alluring Blue

Le Bleu Deux Show Flat - Spa Villa

Mangrove West Coast | Black

Mangrove West Coast | White

Serenade Show Flat

Sinolink Plaza Show Flat - Blue

Sinolink Plaza Show Flat - Red

The Sail at Victoria Show Flat

Hill Paramount

Tai Wai | Hong Kong
Area: 2700 sq ft

Using a nature-based theme, the designer has added a lot of elements relating to the sky as well as forests and rivers. In the living room, these can be found in the waved wall, leaf-shaped stainless steel gate, wall mural, bed headboard… etc.

The designer has used a wealth of materials in the flat to make it look more three-dimensional, such has wallpaper, leather, mirrors, glass and metal. Moreover, different kinds of lights are used to create a variety of layers and moods for the different uses of the flat.

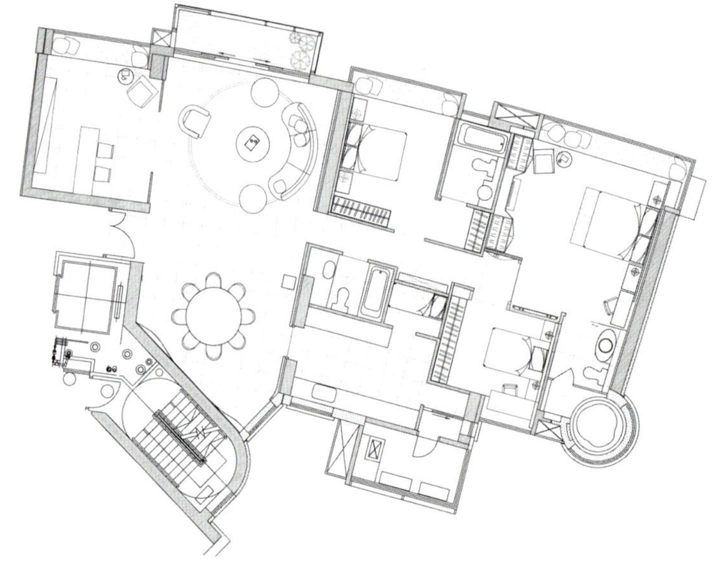

Floor plan

Le Bleu Deux Show Flat - Alluring Blue

Tung Chung | Hong Kong
Area: 950 sq ft

The design scheme created by the client was based on the central colours of green and white. Natural elements like leaves and trees can be found throughout the apartment. Usually designers would use a lot natural materials like bamboo, untreated wood and plants to achieve a natural feeling. In this apartment, however, they are not to be found. Instead there are a lot of tree and leaf graphics together with wallpaper, mirrors, feature walls and accessories containing tree elements. These elements combine well with the modern design of the apartment.

Floor plan

Le Bleu Deux Show Flat - Spa Villa

Tung Chung | Hong Kong
Area: 1800 sq ft + 1800 sq ft roof garden

Upon entering the flat, one is greeted by a spacious, airy living-dining area with floors and walls clad with expanses of white marble. Pieces of classic furniture are scattered throughout the space to accentuate its neutral tone. The dining area is framed by a huge mirror beautifully framed, forming a focal point for the apartment.

The bedrooms are decorated with big floral graphics. Carpeted floors, leather walls and accessories contain floral elements. These are coherently matched with the earth tones in the interior design scheme.

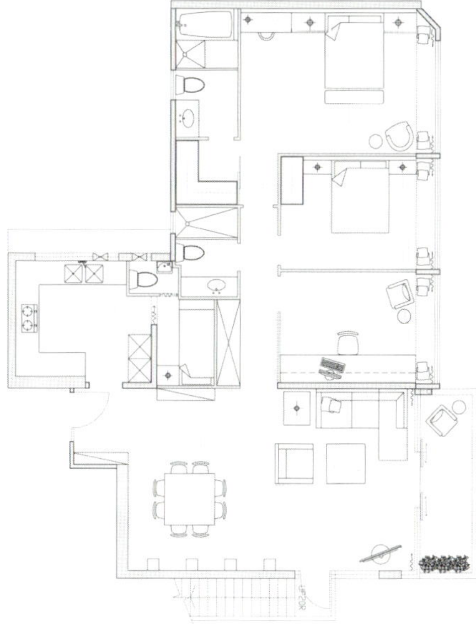

Floor plan

Mangrove West Coast | Black

Shenzhen | China
Area: 1800 sq ft

The use of black, grey, white and beige creates a stylish, cool background for this unit. The spectacular views of the coast are harnessed and continued in the matching interior. Soft materials like sofas, chairs and carpets form warm elements in this cool atmosphere.

A similar approach is adopted in the bedroom where the same level of attention to detail can be found. The use of leather and specially designed lighting effects create an astounding feel and a wonderful place for relaxing.

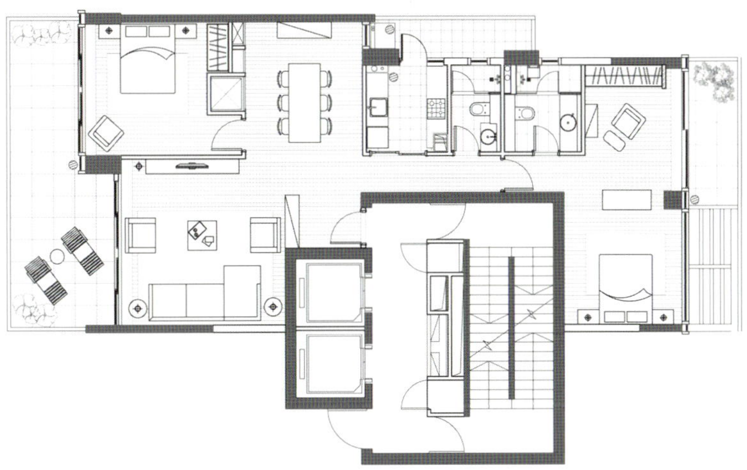

Floor plan

Mangrove West Coast | White

Shenzhen | China
Area: 1500 sq ft

To leave an impression on all visitors, the designer chose a floral theme for this flat. Flower graphics and patterns can be found everywhere in the walls, glass elements, accessories, etc. This fresh feeling is reinforced by a combination of bright red and white colours. Red cushions, chairs, and artwork are the focal points in the flat.

Floral graphics create shadows and add layers to the plain walls. Bird graphics line the corridor acting as a guide to the bedrooms. The floral theme continues in the bedrooms in the bedding, artwork and wall graphics, creating a warm yet refreshing atmosphere.

Wallpaper*

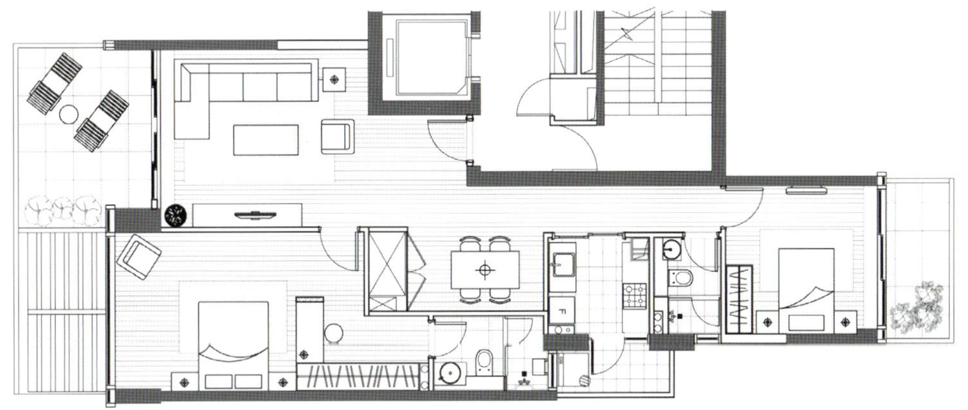

Floor plan

LSA

Serenade Show Flat

Tai Hang | Hong Kong
Area: 3600 sq ft

Occupying the whole 68th floor of the building, this flat consists of living and dining spaces, a family room and three bedrooms, as well as a 200 sq ft terrace. The dwelling area is wrapped around the main service core of the building – lift lobby, service areas, stairwells, etc., thus boasting a 360-degree view to the north of Hong Kong Island.

The sky terrace – which connects the separate living and dining areas – highlights the scenery of Victoria Park and Victoria Harbour. The designer has placed a mural along the corridor to create a continuum throughout the whole area. In another corridor, different-coloured triangular leather panels are combined to create a wall with layers and three-dimensional feel.

In the master bedroom, the designer has removed the wall separating the closet area, replacing it with a glass wardrobe, visually enlarging the space and creating a modern contemporary atmosphere.

The designer has used a variety of wall coverings – timber panels, leather panels, wallpaper, marble and mirrors – in the different areas to create a rich feeling. Every piece of material and accessory has been specially selected by the designer. Entering the apartment is like visiting a museum.

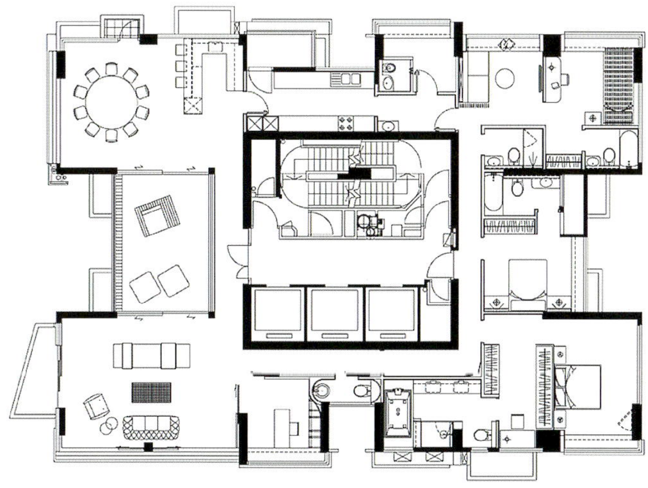

Floor plan

THE STYLE DIARIES

Sinolink Plaza Show Flat - Blue

Shenzhen | China
Area: 1400 sq ft

This flat combines sea blue and brown in a palette with an undeniably relaxed feel. Tempered by dark timbers, natural weaves and some tried-and-tested classic mid-century furniture pieces, the house's heritage is evident, but in this incarnation, it feels as if it has been dressed for a day at the beach.

Rugs in subtle hues mimicking the colours of the surroundings are combined with a mixed array of furniture in natural tones. Artwork has been chosen so as not to compete with the impressive views from the windows.

Colony

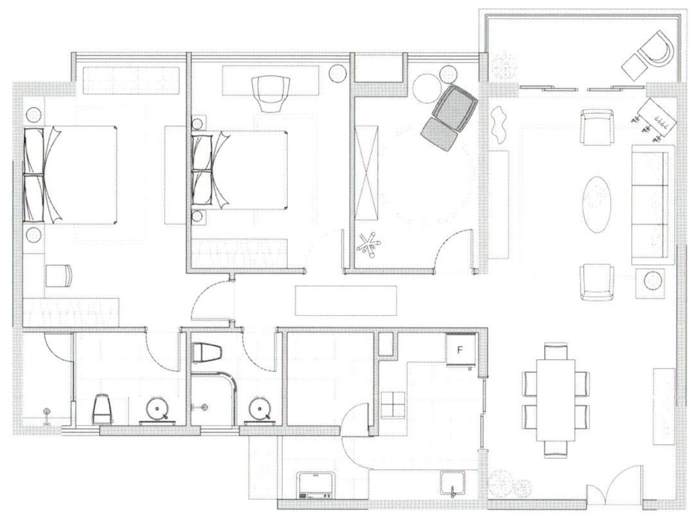

Floor plan

RACING
America's Cup

Sinolink Plaza Show Flat - Red

Shenzhen | China
Area: 1600 sq ft

To create an ideal living space for an architect couple, the most challenging task was to integrate architectural elements into the interior design. In the living area, the designers put bright colours and graphics in the spaces and furniture. Lines and geometric accessories merge to form a strong visual impact.

To avoid creating harsh lines and graphics, the designers used fabrics and French graphics to create a restful ambience.

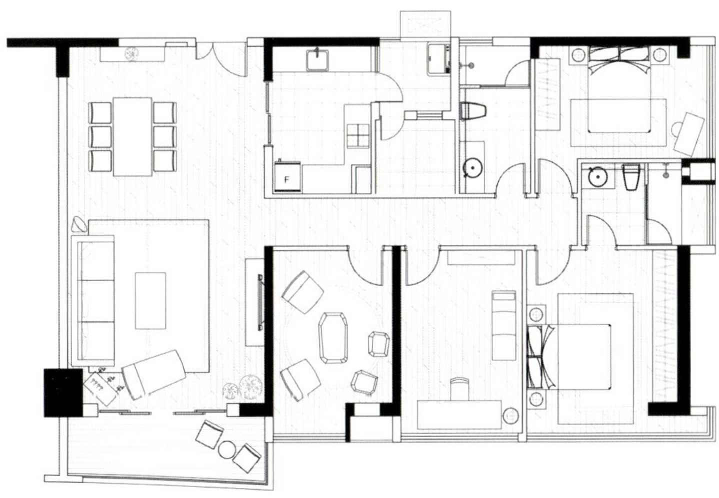

Floor plan

The Sail at Victoria Show Flat

Victoria Road | Hong Kong
Area: 680 sq ft

With a green-free "tree" theme in this apartment, the designers placed a wealth of visual elements in this flat. The dining table, chair, lamp, wall and shelves are all are "plant" species.

Strong colours and graphics have been used in the apartment to create a contrast. As the apartment is tiny, the designers replaced the bedroom wall with a glass partition and used a slim glass wardrobe. All the furniture has been tailor-made to make optimal use of the space.

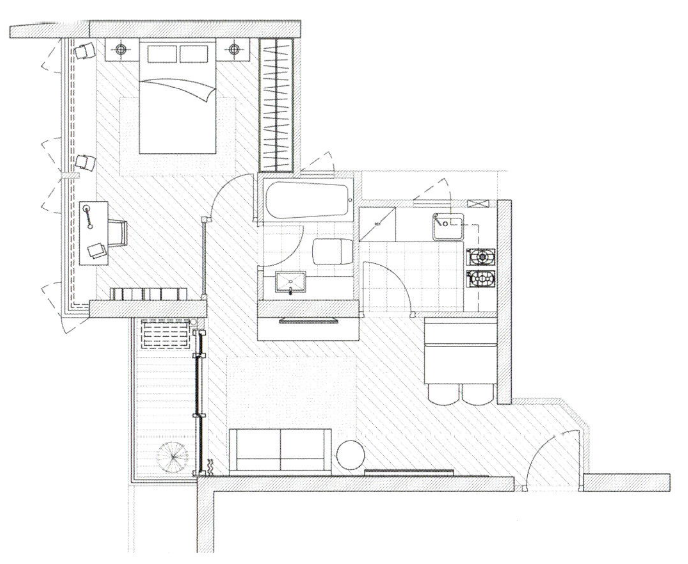

Floor plan